Birth and Early Years of Gandhiji's Life

Mahatma Gandhi is one of the most revered names in Indian history. He was the political and ideological leader of India, also honoured as Father of our nation, he became an international symbol of the free India. He played a very important role in the Indian freedom movement. He is lovingly called as Bapu. His teachings of 'Ahinsa' and 'Satya' (non-violence and truth) changed the complete outlook of the Indian freedom fighters.

Mohan Das Karamchand Gandhi, also known as Mahatma Gandhi, was born on 2nd October 1869 in a Hindu family of Porbandar, Gujarat. His parents were Karamchand Gandhi and Putlibai.

His father, Karamchand Gandhi was a Diwan (Chief Minister) of Porbandar and an honourable and upright man. Gandhiji's mother was a religious and pious woman. Gandhiji gained high moral and social values from his parents. Since childhood, Gandhiji believed strongly in non-violence, truth, purity and very simple lifestyle.

At the age of 13, Gandhiji got married to a girl of the same age named, Kasturba Gandhi. They had four sons. Gandhiji started his education in Porbandar. He further studied in Rajkot and did his matriculation. Then, he joined the University of Bombay in 1887. His family wanted him to become a barrister.

In 1888, he went to London for further studies and completed his law in 1891. He returned to India. For the next two years, he practised law in India.

Gandhiji in South Africa

At the age of 23, Gandhiji left his family once again and came to South Africa as a legal advisor of an Indian businessman. In South Africa, Gandhiji found that there was a strong demarcation between the Black and White communities. The Black community faced a lot of discrimination and were very badly treated. Gandhiji felt very bad about this.

Just after a week of his stay, Gandhiji experienced the humiliation because of discrimination. One day, he had to travel in a train. He had a first-class ticket with him. At the Pietermartizburg station when he entered the first-class compartment and was asked to shift to the third-class compartment. The ticket checker told him that the first-class was reserved for Whites.

On raising objection on this discrimination, Gandhiji was thrown out of the train.

During this journey, he late came to know that discrimination is the common practise there. The Black community and the Indians were called 'coolies'.

After this incident, Gandhiji decided to fight against this injustice. He wrote letters to the higher officials and began a protest against the discrimination in South Africa.

For the next three years, Gandhiji continuously fought for the justice. Soon, he became a well-known activist and a leader of the Indian community.

On 22nd May 1894, Gandhiji established an organisation—Natal Indian Congress (NIC) in South Africa. This organisation looked after the rights of Indians living there. While working for NIC, Gandhiji also faced a lot of opposition from the other communities. He was also attacked several times.

Gandhiji spent twenty years in South Africa. Thereafter, in the year 1915, he returned to India.

Gandhiji in India

Gandhiji's struggles and successes in South Africa were well known in India also. He became a 'National Hero' in the eyes of Indians. Gandhiji wanted to create the same wave of reformation in India. He travelled to all the parts of India to know the real conditions of Indians.

While his travels, Gandhiji used to wear a dhoti and wooden slippers. He renounced all the pleasures and adopted a very simple lifestyle.

He established the 'Sabarmati Ashram' in Ahmedabad,
Gujarat. He lived in the ashram with his family and some
of his supporters. Everyone loved and supported Gandhiji.

People started believing in his teachings
of non-violence and truth. He got the title of
'Mahatma', which meant 'a great soul'.

The Indian Freedom Movement

India was under British rule at that time. A large number of freedom fighters were fighting for the freedom of India. Gandhiji also wanted the freedom of India but he followed a different path. He began a non-violent movement called 'Satyagraha' against the British.

Satyagraha means opposition, but not in an aggressive form. Gandhiji taught people to ask for justice in a silent way. The movement created a strong wave and became a great success.

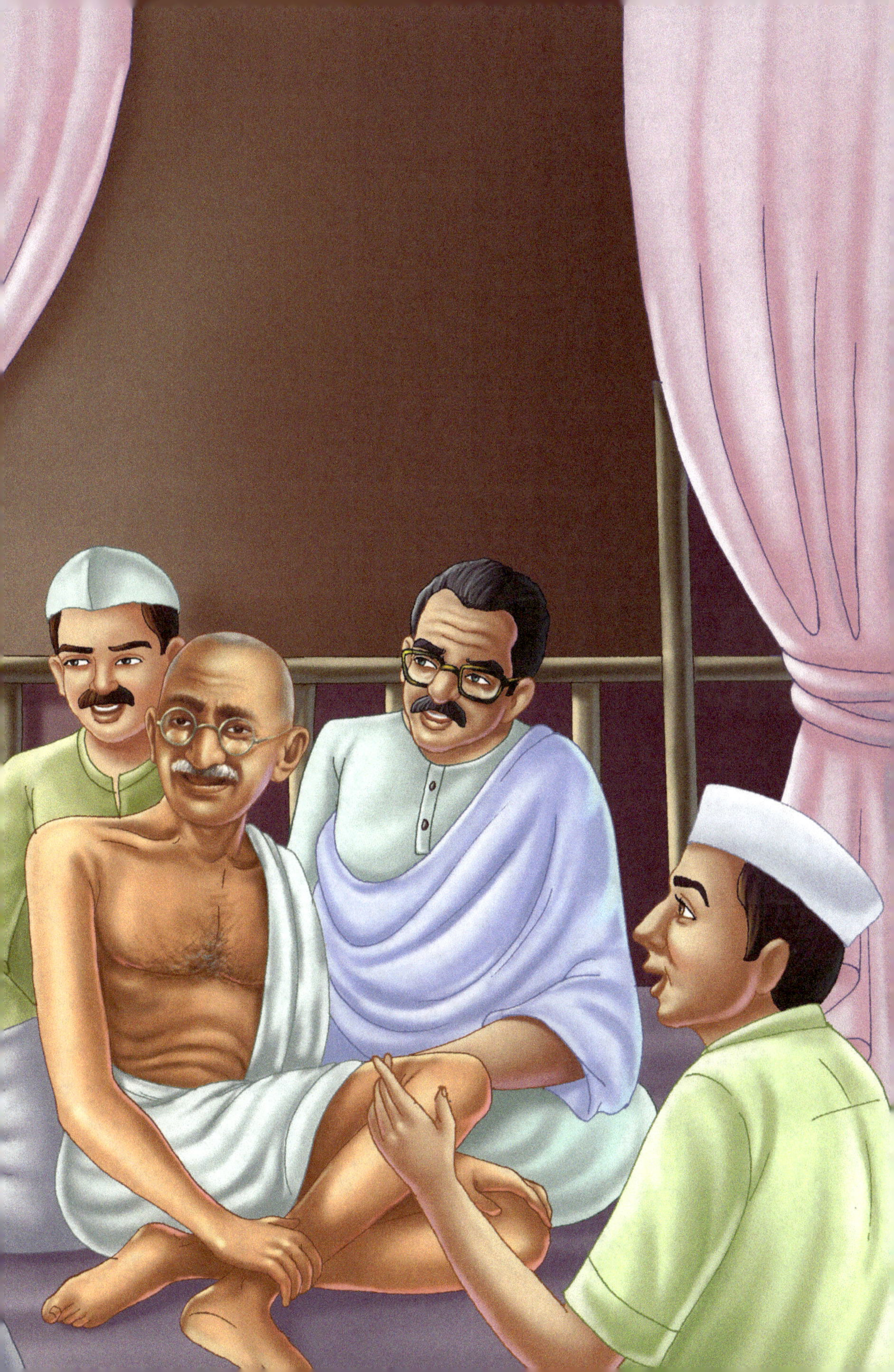

In 1919-20, Gandhiji started another movement called 'Non-cooperative movement'. During his struggle for freedom, Gandhiji was sent to jail many times by the British Govt, but he continued his mission. He asked indians to stop using foreign clothes and other things. He insisted to spin natural cloth on Charkha (spinning wheel). The image of the Charkha later became a symbol of the Indian independence.

On 12th March 1930, Gandhi ji began 'Dandi March' or the 'Salt March' against the salt tax. Gandhi ji with his supporters stand walking 200 miles from Sabarmati Ashram towards the sea.

On April 5, the group reached Dandi, a place along the Coast. Gandhiji demonstrated the method to make salt from the seawater. Soon, the movement spread in the entire nation. Gandhiji was imprisoned once again but, the protest continued nationwide. It was stopped only after the 'Delhi Pact' between the British Government and Gandhiji. The Pact granted the limited salt production and all the protestors were released.

In 1942, Gandhiji issued the last call for independence from British rule. He initiated another movement called 'August Kranti.' Soon after, he began 'Quit India' movement that asked the Britishers to leave India.

After the long struggle and sacrifices, India became independent on 15th August 1947. At the time of freedom, India faced the partition in two parts. After the freedom, Gandhiji tried to maintain peace and unity among the people of different communities.

There was a lot of disturbance in all the parts of country. The communal violence was spreading fast. To stop this violence, Gandhiji began a 'fast unto death' on 13th January 1948 which proved to be a success. On 18th January 1948, he ended his fast only when he got the assurance that the communal violence would be stopped.

Assassination of Gandhiji

Some Indians believed that Gandhiji was responsible for the partition of India. Gandhiji faced a lot of opposition. On the unfortunate day of 30th January 1948, Gandhiji was going to address a prayer meeting. He was walking along with his two assistants—Abha and Manu. Just when he was stepping towards the stage to address the public, a man named Nathuram Godse fired at Gandhiji. Gandhiji fell on the ground, saying, "Hey Ram, Hey Ram!" These were the last words of Mahatma Gandhi.

The great soul, the light of the nation, was gone. The whole country was mourning bitterly on their dear Bapu's departure from the world. The other countries were also shocked at his death.

Soon after the assassination of Mahatma Gandhi, Pt. Jawahar Lal Nehru addressed the nation on radio:
"Friends & Comarades, The light has gone out of our lives and there is darkness everywhere. I do not know what to tell you and how to say it. Our beloved leader, Bapu as we called him, the Father of the Nation, is no more.
Perhaps I am wrong to say that. Nevertheless, we will never see him again as we have seen him for these many years. We will not run to him for advice and seek solace from him, and that is a terrible blow, not only to me, but also to millions and millions in this country.
And it is a little difficult to soften the blow by any other advice that I or anyone else can give you.."

India Remembers Mahatma Gandhi

Mahatma Gandhi's Samadhi is at Raj Ghat in Delhi. Thousands of people from all over the country come to Raj Ghat to pay homage to the great man.

2nd October, Gandhiji's birthday is celebrated as 'Gandhi Jayanti'. It is one of the three National festivals of India. People of India still remember their dear 'Bapu' with great love and reverence.

Every year, 30th January—the day of Gandhiji's assassination, is observed as the Martyr's Day to commemorate the struggle of all those who sacrificed their life for the country. Mahatma Gandhi's picture is also printed on the Indian currency notes.

Mahatma Gandhi was a great writer also. He wrote and edited many newspaper articles during his lifetime. He also wrote several books including his autobiography— My Experiments with Truth.

In the year 1930, Time magazine named Mahatma Gandhi as 'The Man of the Year'. There are many books written about him and his teachings. The life of Mahatma Gandhi has been widely portrayed in the Indian literature, theatre and movies.

Mahatma Gandhi dedicated his entire life for the welfare of Indians. He has been the greatest source of inspiration for all the Indians. His teachings of non-violence, peace and truth are still practised and followed by many, not only in India but also in other countries.

The only way to pay tribute to the great man—The Father of Our Nation—is to follow his teachings in our lives. We should learn from the great life of Mahatma Gandhi.

Dr Sarvapalli Radhakrishnan
The Great Indian Philosopher

Dr Sarvapalli Radhakrishnan is known to be a great thinker, philosopher, educationist, scholar and statesman of India. His birthday, 5th September, is celebrated in India as Teachers' Day every year. He was the first Vice President of India from the year 1952 to 1962. And in 1962, he was elected as the second President of India.

Birth and Early Years of
Dr S. Radhakrishnan's Life

Dr S. Radhakrishnan was born on 5th September 1888 in a town named Tiruttani in Tamilnadu, 84 Kms. to the North West Madras (now Chennai) in a poor Telugu Brahmin family. His parents were Sarvapalli Veeraswami and Sitamma.

His father was a subordinate revenue official in the service of a local Zamindar (landlord).

Dr S. Radhakrishnan got his primary education at a high school in Tiruttani. His parents recognised his talents and tried their best to give him good education. In 1896, he was moved to the Hermansburg Evangelical Lutheral Mission School in Tirupati.

Dr S. Radhakrishnan was a brilliant student. He received many scholarships and awards in his student life. He joined Voorheese College in Vellore. Then, he joined Madras Christian College. In 1906, he got his postgraduate degree in Philosophy from there.

Dr S. Radhakrishnan's family had many financial constraints. He studied Philosophy by chance and not by choice. He got the books of Philosophy from one of his elder cousins who passed out from the same college. So, he decided to study the subject. But later on, he got very much interested in the subject and wrote many acclaimed works in Philosophy.

When Dr S. Radhakrishnan was 16-years old, he got married to his distant cousin named Sivakamu. The couple had five daughters and a son.

Professional Life of Dr S. Radhakrishnan

In 1909, he was appointed at the Department of Philosophy in Madras Presidency College. Thereafter in 1918, he was appointed as a professor of Philosophy in the University of Mysore.

Dr S. Radhakrishnan wrote many articles in Philosophy journals. He was highly influenced by the teachings of Rabindra Nath Tagore. His first book was 'The Philosophy of Rabindra Nath Tagore'. The second book that he wrote was 'The Reign of Religion in Contemporary Philosophy'.

In the year 1921, Dr S. Radhakrishnan got the chair of King George V, as the Professor of Philosophy at the Department of Mental and Moral Science in the University of Calcutta. He represented the University of Calcutta at the Congress of Universities in the British Empire 1926. He also represented the University at the International Congress of Philosophy at Harvard University in the same year.

In 1929, Dr S. Radhakrishnan was invited to deliver a lecture at Harris Manchester College, Oxford. His lecture was soon published in the form of a book, 'An Idealist View of Life'.

And soon, he was invited to take post of Principal at Harris Manchester College. During this period, he got an opportunity to deliver many important lectures. He created a bridge between East and West and explained the philosophical systems of all the traditions to people.

Dr S. Radhakrishnan acted as the Vice Chancellor
of Andhra University from 1931 to 1936. In the year 1936,
he was elected as a fellow of All Souls College. He was
named as the 'Spalding Professor of Eastern Religions and
Ethics' at Oxford University.

In 1939, Pt. Madan Mohan Malviya invited
Dr S. Radhakrishnan to succeed him as a Vice Chancellor of
the Banaras Hindu University (BHU). He worked at BHU till
January 1948.

After India's independence in 1947, Dr S. Radhakrishnan represented the country at UNESCO. Later, he also acted as the Ambassador of India to Soviet Union. He was also elected to the Constituent Assembly of India.

In 1952, Dr S. Radhakrishnan was elected as the first Vice President of India. He became the President of India in the year 1962. He occupied the honourable position till 1967.

When Dr S. Radhakrishnan became the President of India, the entire world was pleased. He was one of the greatest philosophers of the world, Bertrand Russell said,

"It is an honour to Philosophy that Dr S. Radhakrishnan is the President of India and I, as a philosopher, take special pleasure in this. Pleto aspired for philosophers to become kings and it is a tribute to India to have a philosopher as a President.

Even working on the post of the President, Dr S. Radhakrishnan was extremely humble. During his work tenure, people from all the sections of society were welcome at Rashtrapati Bhavan. He listened to each and every person and addressed all the issues. He tried his best to resolve the issues of the society.

Dr S. Radhakrishnan wrote many significant books on Indian traditions and culture. He popularised the greatness of Indian traditions, teachings and Hinduism in western countries.

Dr S. Radhakrishnan earned many prestigious honours and titles for his extraordinary services in the field of education. He was honoured by the knighthood in 1931. He was also honoured by the Bharat Ratna in 1954, and the Order of Merit in 1963.

In 1961, Dr S. Radhakrishnan received the Peace Prize of the German Book Trade. He also received the Templeton Prize in 1975. He donated the entire amount of the Templeton Prize to the Oxford University. In 1989, the University started giving 'Dr S. Radhakrishnan scholarships' in his memory. Many authors and educationists all around the world were influenced by Dr S. Radhakrishnan and his philosophies. There are also some books written on his life and his ideas.

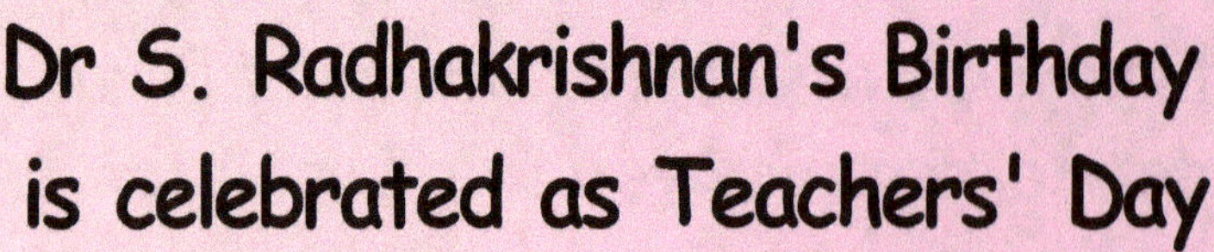

Dr S. Radhakrishnan's Birthday
is celebrated as Teachers' Day

Dr S. Radhakrishnan said, "The teachers should be the best minds of the country." In his opinion, teachers should not only instruct the students but also earn their affection. He also believed that respect for teachers should be earned, not demanded.

Dr S. Radhakrishnan not only imparted knowledge to his students but also earned their true love and respect for his unique style of teachings. He was very popular among the students.

TEACHER'S DAY

When Dr S. Radhakrishnan was leaving the University of Mysore, his students organised a grand farewell for him. He was taken to the railway station in a flower-decked carriage pulled by his students.

There is an interesting incident about how the celebration of Teachers' Day started on Dr S. Radhakrishnan's birthday. When he was elected as the President of India, some of his students asked for his permission to celebrate his birthday.

Dr S. Radhakrishnan believed that teachers play a very important role in shaping the future of the students and the country.

Dr S. Radhakrishnan said to his students, "Instead of celebrating my birthday separately, it would be my proud privilege if September 5 will be observed as Teachers' Day." He asked his students to dedicate "Teachers' Day" not only to him but also to all the teachers.

Since then every year, Dr S. Radhakrishnan's birthday, 5th September, is celebrated as Teachers' Day all across the country. All the schools, colleges and institutions celebrate the day in the honour of the great man and all the teachers.

Dr S. Radhakrishnan regarded the teaching as the noblest profession. He believed that the progress of any nation depends largely on the teachers. Teachers dedicate their lives to educate their students.

He once said, "The aim of education is not the acquisition of information, although important, or acquisition of technical skills, though essential in modern society but the development of that bent of mind, that attitude of reason, that spirit of democracy which will make us responsible citizens."

Last Years of Dr S. Radhakrishnan's Life

Dr S. Radhakrishnan retired from the public life in 1967. He spent the last years of his life in his house in Madras (Chennai). He breathed his last at the age of 87 on 17th April 1975.

His death was a big loss for the country. His absence created a vacuum in the field of education and philosophy. He is still remembered for his valuable work all over the world. His birthday is celebrated with great enthusiasm as Teachers' Day all across India.

Dr S. Radhakrishnan dedicated his whole life in educating and empowering people. His only motto was to make India a wonderful nation standing on a strong foundation of education. He believed that only education could change and shape the future of the entire nation.

We can learn a lot from the great life of Dr S. Radhakrishnan. We should always remember his significance and efforts in keeping the foundation of the Indian education system.

www.ingramcontent.com/pod-product-compliance
Lightning Source LLC
LaVergne TN
LVHW080050210726
843507LV00017B/871